Quick and Easy Flavorful Recipes

for the Mediterranean Diet

Elisa R. Grande

Contents

Chapter One

Simple Greek Salad

Time Required for Preparation: 15 minutes Time Required for Cooking: 0 minutes 2 portions Difficulty Easy

Ingredients:

4 oz cubed Greek feta cheese f 5 cucumbers, cut lengthwise f 1 teaspoon honey f 1 lemon, chewed and grated f 1 cup pitted and halved kalamata olives f 14 cup extra virgin olive oil f 1 onion, sliced f 1 teaspoon oregano f 1 pinch fresh oregano (for garnish) f 12 tomatoes, quartered

Directions:

Soak the onions in salted water for 15 minutes in a bowl. Combine the honey, lemon juice, lemon peel, oregano, salt, and pepper in a large bowl. Combine all ingredients. Add the olive oil gradually, beating constantly, until the oil emulsifies. Combine the olives and tomatoes in a medium bowl. Correct it. Combine the cucumbers

Drain and add the onions that have been soaked in salted water to the salad mixture. Fresh oregano and feta cheese should be sprinkled on top of the salad. Drizzle with olive oil and season with freshly ground pepper to taste.

Nutritional information (per 100g): 292 kcal 17g Carbohydrates 12g Fat Protein: 6 g Sodium 743mg

Salad with Arugula, Figs, and Walnuts

15 minutes for preparation Time Required for Cooking: 10 minutes 2 portions

Difficulty Easy

Ingredients:

5 oz arugula f 1 scraped carrot f 1/8 teaspoon cayenne pepper f 3 oz crumbled goat cheese f 1 can salt-free chickpeas 12 cup dried figs, peeled and cut into wedges 1 teaspoon honey 3 tablespoons olive oil 2 teaspoons balsamic vinegar 12 walnuts, halved

Directions:

Preheat oven to 175 degrees Fahrenheit. Combine the nuts, 1 tablespoon olive oil, cayenne pepper, and 1/8 teaspoon salt in a baking dish. Bake the baking sheet until the nuts are brown. When you are finished, set it away.

Combine the honey, balsamic vinegar, 2 tablespoons oil, and 34 teaspoon salt in a bowl.

Combine the arugula, carrots, and figs in a large bowl. Drizzle with balsamic honey vinaigrette and top with nuts and goat cheese. Ascertain that you have covered everything.

Nutritional information (per 100g): 403 kcal 9g Carbohydrates 35g Fat 844mg Sodium 13g Protein

Cauliflower Salad with Tahini Vinaigrette 15 minutes to prepare Time Required for Cooking: 5 minutes 2 portions Difficulty Average

f 12 pound cauliflower f 14 cup dried cherries f 3 tablespoons lemon juice f 1 tablespoon chopped fresh mint f 1 teaspoon olive oil f 12 cup chopped parsley f 3 tablespoons chopped roasted salted pistachios f 12 teaspoon salt f 14 cup chopped shallot f 2 tablespoons tahini

Directions:

In a microwave-safe container, combine the cauliflower, olive oil, and 14 salt. Ensure that you cover and

Evenly season the cauliflower. Wrap the bowl in plastic wrap and microwave for about 3 minutes.

Arrange the rice and cauliflower on a baking sheet and let to cool for about 10 minutes. Combine the lemon juice and shallots in a small bowl. Enable it to sit for a few minutes to allow the cauliflower to absorb the flavor.

Combine the tahini, cherries, parsley, mint, and salt in a small bowl. Combine everything well. Before serving, sprinkle with roasted pistachios.

Nutritional information (per 100g): 165 kcal 10g Carbohydrates 20g Fat 6 grams protein 651 milligrams sodium

Mediterranean Potato Salad Time Required for Preparation: 15 minutes Time Required for Cooking: 10 minutes 2 Servings Difficulty Level: Simple

1 bunch torn basil leaves f 1 smashed garlic clove f 1 tablespoon olive oil f 1 sliced onion f 1 teaspoon oregano f 100 g roasted red pepper 300g sliced potatoes f 1 can cherry tomatoes f salt and pepper to taste

Directions:

In a saucepan, sauté the onions. Combine the oregano and garlic. He quickly prepares everything. Combine the pepper and tomatoes in a medium bowl. Season to taste, then boil for about 10 minutes. Leave it to one side.

Boil the potatoes in salted water in a saucepan. Cook until the vegetables are soft, approximately 15 minutes. Drain thoroughly. Combine the potatoes and sauce, along with the basil and olives. Finally, before serving, discard everything.

111 calories per 100g 9g Carbohydrates 16g Fat 745mg Sodium 3g Protein

Salad with Quinoa and Pistachios Time Required for Preparation: 10 minutes Time Required for Cooking: 15 minutes 2 Servings Difficulty Level: Simple

14 teaspoon cumin f 12 cup dried currants f 1 teaspoon grated lemon zest f 2 tablespoons lemon juice f 12 cup chopped green onions f 1 tablespoon chopped mint f 2 tablespoons extra virgin olive oil f 14 cup chopped parsley f 14 teaspoon ground pepper f 1/3 cup chopped pistachios

Directions:

1. Combine 1 2/3 cup water, raisins, and quinoa in a saucepan. Bring to a boil and then lower to a low heat. Allow around 10 minutes for the quinoa to get frothy. Set aside for about 5 minutes. Transfer the quinoa mixture to a container. Combine the almonds, mint, onions, and parsley in a medium bowl. Combine all ingredients. Combine the lemon zest, lemon juice, currants, cumin, and oil in a separate bowl. They should be beaten jointly. Combine the dry and wet ingredients in a mixing bowl.

Nutritional information (per 100g): 248 kcal 8g Carbohydrates 35g Fat Protein: 7 g Sodium 914mg

Salad with Cucumber and Chicken with Spicy Peanut Dressing

15 minutes for preparation Time Required for Cooking: 0 minutes 2 portions

Difficulty Average

Ingredients:\sf 1 tablespoon sambal oelek (chili paste) 1 tablespoon low-sodium soy sauce 1 teaspoon toasted sesame oil 4 tablespoons water, or more if required 1 cucumber, peeled and thinly sliced 1 cooked chicken fillet, shredded into thin strips

Directions:

1. In a mixing dish, combine peanut butter, soy sauce, sesame oil, sambal oelek, and water. Arrange the cucumber slices in a single layer on a serving plate. Serve garnished with grated chicken and sauce. Sprinkle chopped peanuts on top.

Nutritional information (per 100g): 720 kcal 54 g triglycerides 9 g carbs Contains 9g protein sodium 733mg

German Hot Potato Salad Time Required for Preparation: 10 minutes Time Required for Cooking: 30 minutes 12 portions

Average Difficulty

9 peeled potatoes f 6 bacon slices f 1/8 teaspoon minced black pepper f 1/2 teaspoon celery seed f 2 tablespoons white sugar f 2 teaspoons salt f 3/4 cup water f 1/3 cup distilled white vinegar f 2 tablespoons all-purpose flour

Directions:

In a big saucepan, bring salted water to a boil. Cook until the potatoes are tender but still firm, approximately 30 minutes.

Drain, cool, and slice finely. Cook bacon in a pan over medium heat. Prepare by draining, crumbling, and reserving. Make a note of the cooking liquids. Cook onions till golden brown in bacon oil.

In a small bowl, whisk together flour, sugar, salt, celery seed, and pepper. Cook, stirring constantly, until the sautéed onions are bubbly, then remove from heat. Stir in the water and vinegar, then return the pan to the heat and bring to a boil, continually stirring. Bring to a boil and stir. Add the bacon and potato slices gradually to the vinegar/water combination, gently stirring until the potatoes are warmed through.

205 calories per 100g 5 g triglycerides 9 g carbs 814mg sodium 3g protein

Salad de Fiesta de Pollo

Time Required for Preparation: 20 minutes Time Required for Cooking: 20 minutes 4 portions Difficulty Easy

Ingredients:\sf 2 chicken fillet halves, skin and bones removed 1 fajitas herb package, split 1 tablespoon vegetable oil f 1 can washed and drained black beans f 1 package corn in the Mexican style f 1/2 cup salsa f 1 packet green salad f 1 chopped onion 1 quartered tomato

Directions:

1. Rub 1/2 of the herbs for fajitas evenly over the chicken. In a frying pan over medium heat, heat the oil and cook the chicken for 8 minutes on each side or until the juices run clear; set aside. In a large skillet, combine the beans, corn, salsa, and remaining 1/2 fajita seasonings. Bring to a simmer over medium heat and cook until lukewarm. Combine green veggies, onion, and tomato in a salad bowl. Dress the beans and corn mixture and cover the chicken salad.

311 calories per 100g 2g carbs 4g fat 853mg sodium 23g protein

Salad with Corn and Black Beans Preparation Time: 10 minutes Time Required for Cooking: 0 minutes 4 portions

Level of Difficulty: Easy

Ingredients:

2 tbsp vegetable oil

1/4 cup balsamic vinaigrette

1 tsp. salt 1 tsp. white sugar

1/2 teaspoon cumin powder

1 teaspoon freshly ground black pepper

1 tsp chili powder

3 tablespoons fresh coriander, diced 1 can black beans (15 oz)

1 can (75 oz) sweetened corn, drained

Directions:

1. In a small bowl, whisk together balsamic vinegar, oil, salt, sugar, black pepper, cumin, and chili powder. In a medium bowl, combine black corn and beans. Combine with vinaigrette of vinegar and oil and garnish with coriander. Refrigerate overnight.

214 calories per 100g 4 g triglycerides 6 g carbs 5 grams protein 415 milligrams sodium

Salad with Pasta

30 minutes for preparation Time Required for Cooking: 10 minutes 16 portions

Average Difficulty

1 (16-oz) package fusilli pasta f 3 cups cherry tomatoes f 1/2 pound diced provolone f 1/2 pound diced sausage f 1/4 pound pepperoni, cut in half 1 large green pepper f 1 drained can of black olives f 1 jar of drained chilis (8 oz) vinaigrette italiana

Directions:

In a saucepan, bring lightly salted water to a boil. Stir in the pasta and cook for about 8 to 10 minutes or until al dente. Drain and rinse with cold water.

Combine pasta with tomatoes, cheese, salami, pepperoni, green pepper, olives, and peppers in a large bowl. Pour the vinaigrette and mix well.

Nutritional information (per 100g): 310 calories 7g fat 9g carbohydrates Contains 9g protein 746mg sodium

Rice with Vermicelli

Preparation Time : 5 minutes

Cooking Time : 45 minutes

Servings : 6

Difficulty Grading: Simple

Ingredients:\sf 2 cups short-grain rice\sf 3½ cups water, plus more for rinsing and soaking the rice\sf ¼ cup olive oil\sf 1 cup broken vermicelli pasta\sf Salt

Directions:

Soak the rice under cold water until the water runs clean. Place the rice in a bowl, cover with water, and let soak for 10 minutes. Drain and set aside. Cook the olive oil in a medium pot over medium heat.

Stir in the vermicelli and cook for 2 to 3 minutes, stirring continuously, until golden.

Put the rice and cook for 1 minute, stirring, so the rice is well coated in the oil. Stir in the water and a pinch of salt and bring the liquid to a boil. Adjust heat and simmer for 20 minutes. Pull out from the heat and let rest for 10 minutes. Fluff with a fork and serve.

Nutritional information per 100g 346 calories 9g total fat 60g carbohydrates 2g protein 9mg sodium

Chapter Two

Fava Beans and Rice\s

Preparation Time : 10 minutes

Cooking Time : 35 minutes

4 portion

Difficulty Grading: Simple

Ingredients:\sf ¼ cup olive oil\sf 4 cups fresh fava beans, shelled\sf 4½ cups water, plus more for drizzling

f 2 cups basmati rice\sf 1/8 teaspoon salt\sf 1/8 teaspoon freshly ground black pepper\sf 2 tablespoons pine nuts, toasted\sf ½ cup chopped fresh garlic chives, or fresh onion chives

Directions:

Fill the sauce pan with olive oil and cook over medium heat. Add the fava beans and drizzle them with a bit of water to avoid burning or sticking. Cook for 10 minutes.

Gently stir in the rice. Add the water, salt, and pepper. Set up the heat and boil the mixture. Adjust the heat and let it simmer for 15 minutes.

Pull out from the heat and let it rest for 10 minutes before serving. Spoon onto a serving platter and sprinkle with the toasted pine nuts and chives.

Nutritional information per 100g 587 calories 17g total fat 97g carbohydrates 2g protein 6mg sodium

Buttered Fava Beans

30 minutes for pre-preparation 15 minutes total cook time 4 portion

Difficulty Grading: Simple

Ingredients:\sf ½ cup vegetable broth\sf 4 pounds fava beans, shelled\sf ¼ cup fresh tarragon, divided\sf 1 teaspoon chopped fresh thyme f ¼ teaspoon freshly ground black pepper f 1/8 teaspoon salt\sf 2 tablespoons butter\sf 1 garlic clove, minced\sf 2 tablespoons chopped fresh parsley

Directions:

Boil vegetable broth in a shallow pan over medium heat. Add the fava beans, 2 tablespoons of tarragon, the thyme, pepper, and salt. Cook until the broth is almost absorbed and the beans are tender.

Stir in the butter, garlic, and remaining 2 tablespoons of tarragon. Cook for 2 to 3 minutes. Sprinkle with the parsley and serve hot.

Nutritional information per 100g 458 calories 9g fat 81g carbohydrates 37g protein 691mg sodium

Freekeh\sPreparation Time : 10 minutes

Cooking Time : 40 minutes

4 portion

Difficulty Grading: Simple

Ingredients:\sf 4 tablespoons Ghee\sf 1 onion, chopped\sf 3½ cups vegetable broth f 1 teaspoon ground allspice f 2 cups freekeh\sf 2 tablespoons pine nuts, toasted

Directions:\s1. Melt ghee in a heavy-bottomed saucepan over medium heat. Stir in the onion and cook for about 5 minutes, stirring constantly, until the onion is golden. Pour in the vegetable broth, add the allspice, and bring to a boil. Stir in the freekeh and return the mixture to a boil. Adjust heat and simmer for 30 minutes, stir occasionally. Spoon the freekeh into a serving dish and top with the toasted pine nuts.

Nutritional information per 100g 459 calories 18g fat 64g carbohydrates 10g protein 692mg sodium

Feta Chicken Burgers

Preparation Time : 10 minutes

30 minutes for cooking

Servings : 6\sDifficulty Level : Average\sIngredients:

f ¼ cup Reduced-fat mayonnaise f ¼ cup Finely chopped cucumber f ¼ tsp Black pepper\sf 1 tsp Garlic powder\sf ½ cup Chopped roasted sweet red pepper\sf ½ tsp Greek seasoning\sf 5 lb. Lean ground chicken f 1 cup Crumbled feta cheese f 6 Whole wheat burger buns

Directions:

Preheat the broiler to the oven ahead of time. Mix the mayo and cucumber. Set aside.

Combine each of the seasonings and red pepper for the burgers. Mix the chicken and the cheese well. Form the mixture into 6 ½-inch thick patties.

Cook the burgers in a broiler and place approximately four inches from the heat source. Cook until the thermometer reaches 165° Fahrenheit.

Serve with buns and cucumber sauce. Garnish with tomato and lettuce if desired and serve.

Nutrition (for 100g): 356 Calories 14g Fat 10g Carbohydrates 31g Protein 691mg Sodium

Roast Pork for Tacos\sPreparation Time : 10 minutes

Cooking Time : 1 hour 15 minutes

Servings : 6

Difficulty Standard of living:

Ingredients:

I Pork shoulder roast (4 lb.)\si Diced green chilies (2 - 4 oz. cans) (2 - 4 oz. cans)

I Chili powder (.25 cup) (.25 cup) I Dried oregano (1 tsp) (1 tsp.) I Taco seasoning (1 tsp.) I Garlic (2 tsp.)\si Salt (5 tsp. or as desired) (5 tsp. or as desired)

Directions:

Set the oven to reach 300° Fahrenheit.

Situate the roast on top of a large sheet of aluminum foil.

Drain the chilis. Mince the garlic.

Mix the green chilis, taco seasoning, chili powder, oregano, and garlic. Rub the mixture over the roast and cover using a layer of foil.

Place the wrapped pork on top of a roasting rack on a cookie sheet to catch any leaks.

Roast it for 5 to 4 hours in the hot oven until it's falling apart. Cook until the center reaches at least 145° Fahrenheit when tested with a meat thermometer (internal temperature) (internal temperature).

Transfer the roast to a chopping block to shred into small pieces using two forks. Season it as desired. Nutritional information per 100g 290 Calories 6g Fat 12g Carbohydrates 3g Protein 471mg Sodium

Italian Apple - Olive Oil Cake\sPreparation Time : 10 minutes

Cooking Time : 1 hour 10 minutes

12 portiones

Difficulty Standard of living:

Ingredients:\sf Gala apples (2 large) (2 large)

f Orange juice - for soaking apples f All-purpose flour (3 cups) (3 cups)

f Ground cinnamon (.5 tsp.) f Nutmeg (.5 tsp.)\sf Baking powder (1 tsp.)\sf Baking soda (1 tsp) (1 tsp.)

f Sugar (1 cup)\sf Olive oil (1 cup) (1 cup)

f Large eggs (2) (2)

f Gold raisins (.66 cup) (.66 cup)

f Confectioner's sugar - for dusting f Also Needed: 9-inch baking pan

Directions:

Peel and finely chop the apples. Drizzle the apples with just enough orange juice to prevent browning.

Soak the raisins in warm water for 15 minutes and drain well.

Sift the baking soda, flour, baking powder, cinnamon, and nutmeg. Set it to the side for now.

Pour the olive oil and sugar into the bowl of a stand mixer. Mix on the low setting for 2 minutes or until well combined.

Blend it while running, break in the eggs one at a time and continue mixing for 2 minutes. The mixture should increase in volume; it should be thick - not runny.

Combine all of the ingredients well. Build hole in the center of the flour mixture and add in the olive and sugar mixture.

Remove the apples of any excess of juice and drain the raisins that have been soaking. Add them together with the batter, mixing well.

Prepare the baking pan with parchment paper. Place the batter onto the pan and level it with the back of a wooden spoon.

Bake it for 45 minutes at a 350° Fahrenheit.

When ready, remove the cake from the parchment paper and place it into a serving dish. Dust with the confectioner's sugar. Heat dark honey to garnish the top.

Nutrition (for 100g): 294 Calories 11g Fat 9g Carbohydrates 3g Protein 691mg Sodium

Speedy Tilapia with Red Onion and Avocado

Preparation Time : 10 minutes

5 minutes for cooking

4 portion

Average Degree of Difficulty

Ingredients:\sf 1 tablespoon extra-virgin olive oil\sf 1 tablespoon freshly squeezed orange juice

f ¼ teaspoon kosher or sea salt\sf 4 (4-ounce) tilapia fillets, more oblong than square, skin-on or skinned\sf ¼ cup chopped red onion\sf 1 avocado

Directions:

In a 9-inch glass pie dish, combine together the oil, orange juice, and salt. Work on the fillet simultaneously, situate each in the pie dish and coat on all sides. Form the fillets in a wagon-wheel formation. Place each fillet with 1 tablespoon of onion, thenfold the end of the fillet that's hanging over the edge in half over the onion. Once done, you should have 4 folded-over fillets with the fold against the outer edge of the dish and the ends all in the center.

Wrap the dish with plastic, leave small part open at the edge to vent the steam. Cook on high for about 3 minutes in microwave. When done it should separate into flakes (chunks) when pressed gently with a fork. Garnish the fillets with the avocado and serve.

Nutrition (for 100g): 200 Calories 3g Fat 4g Carbohydrates 22g Protein 811mg Sodium

Chicken with Caper Sauce Preparation Time : 10 minutes

Cooking Time : 18 minutes

Servings : 5 Difficulty Level : Difficult Ingredients: f For Chicken: f 2 eggs f Salt and ground black pepper, as required f 1 cup dry breadcrumbs f 2 tablespoons olive oil f 1½ pounds skinless, boneless chicken breast halves, pounded into ¾inch thickness and cut into pieces f For Capers Sauce: f 3 tablespoons capers f ½ cup dry white wine f 3 tablespoons fresh lemon juice f Salt and ground black pepper, as required f 2 tablespoons fresh parsley, chopped

For chicken: in a shallow dish, add the eggs, salt and black pepper and beat until well combined. In

another shallow dish, place breadcrumbs. Soak the chicken pieces in egg mixture then coat with the breadcrumbs evenly. Shake off the excess breadcrumbs.

Cook the oil over medium heat and cook the chicken pieces for about 5-7 minutes per side or until desired doneness. With a slotted spoon, situate the chicken pieces onto a paper towel lined plate. With a piece of the foil, cover the chicken pieces to keep them warm.

In the same skillet, incorporate all the sauce ingredients except parsley and cook for about 2-3 minutes, stirring continuously. Mix in the parsley and remove from heat. Serve the chicken pieces with the topping of capers sauce.

Nutrition (for 100g): 352 Calories 5g Fat 9g Carbohydrates 2g Protein 741mg Sodium

Chapter Three

Mango Salsa on Turkey Burgers

15 minutes for preparation

Time Required for Cooking: 10 minutes

6 portions

Difficulty Easy

1 teaspoon sea salt, divided f 14 teaspoon freshly ground black pepper f 2 tablespoons extra-virgin olive oil f 2 mangos, peeled, pitted, and cubed f 12 red onion, finely chopped f 1 lime juice f 1 garlic clove, minced f 12 jalapeo pepper, seeded and finely minced f 2 tablespoons chopped fresh cilantro leaves

Directions:\s1. Form 4 patties from the turkey breast and season with 12 teaspoon sea salt and pepper. In a nonstick skillet, heat the olive oil until it shimmers. Cook the turkey patties for about 5 minutes each side, or until browned.

While the patties are cooking, in a separate bowl, combine the mango, red onion, lime juice, garlic, jalapeo, cilantro, and remaining 12 teaspoon sea salt. Serve the turkey patties with the salsa.

384 calories per 100g 3g Carbohydrates 27g Fat 692mg Sodium 34g Protein

Turkey Roasted with Herbs 15 minutes for breast preparation

Time Required for Cooking: 112 hours (plus 20 minutes to rest)

6 portions

Average Difficulty

Ingredients:\sf 2 tbsp olive oil extra-virgin f 4 minced garlic cloves 1 lemon's zest 1 tablespoon fresh thyme leaves, chopped 1 tablespoon fresh rosemary leaves, chopped 2 tbsp. chopped fresh Italian parsley 1 tsp mustard powder f 1 tsp sea salt f 14 tsp freshly ground black pepper f 1 (6-pound) bone-in, skin-on turkey breast

Directions:

Preheat oven to 325 degrees Fahrenheit. Combine olive oil, garlic, lemon zest, thyme, rosemary, parsley, mustard, sea salt, and pepper in a medium mixing bowl. Brush the herb mixture evenly over the turkey breast, loosening and rubbing the skin below as well. Arrange the turkey breast skin-side up in a roasting pan on a rack.

Fill the pan halfway with wine. Roast for 1 to 112 hours, or until the turkey reaches a temperature of 165 degrees F on the inside. Remove from the oven and put aside for 20 minutes before cutting, tented with aluminum foil to keep warm.

392 calories per 100g 1 g Carbohydrates 2 g Fat Protein: 84g Sodium 741mg

Sausage and Peppers with Chicken

Time Required for Preparation: 10 minutes

Time Required for Cooking: 20 minutes

6 portions

Difficulty Average

2 tablespoons extra-virgin olive oil 6 Italian chicken sausage links 1 onion 1 red bell pepper 1 green bell pepper 3 minced garlic cloves 12 cup dry white wine 12 teaspoon sea salt 14 teaspoon freshly ground black pepper

In a large pan, heat the olive oil until it shimmers. Cook for 5 to 7 minutes before adding the sausages.

Turning periodically, bake until browned and internal temperature reaches 165°F. Remove the sausage from the skillet with tongs and place on a serving plate, tented with aluminum foil to keep warm.

Reintroduce the onion, red bell pepper, and green bell pepper to the pan and stir well. Cook, stirring often, until the veggies start to brown. Cook for 30 seconds, stirring regularly.

Combine the wine, sea salt, pepper, and red pepper flakes in a medium bowl. Take any browned pieces from the bottom of the pan and fold them in. Continue to cook, stirring occasionally, for about 4 minutes more, or until the liquid has reduced by half. Serve the peppers on top of the sausages.

Nutritional information (per 100g): 173 calories 6g Carbohydrates 1g Fat Protein: 22 g Sodium 582mg

Chicken Piccata Time Required for Preparation: 10 minutes

Time Required for Cooking: 15 minutes

6 portions

Difficulty Average

12 cup whole-wheat flour 12 teaspoon sea salt 1/8 teaspoon freshly ground black pepper 112 pound chicken breasts, split into six pieces 3 tbsp extra-virgin olive oil f 12 tbsp dry white wine f 1 cup unsalted chicken broth f 1 lemon's juice 1 lemon's zest f 14 cup capers, drained and washed f 14 cup fresh parsley leaves, chopped

Directions:

Whisk together the flour, sea salt, and pepper in a small bowl. Flour the chicken and tap off excess. Cook until the olive oil shimmers.

Cook the chicken for about 4 minutes each side, or until browned. Remove the chicken from the pan and put aside to keep warm, covered with aluminum foil.

Re-heat the skillet and add the broth, wine, lemon juice, lemon zest, and capers. Scoop and fold in any browned pieces from the pan's bottom using the edge of a spoon. Reduce to a low heat and continue cooking until the liquid thickens. Remove the skillet from the heat and reintroduce the chicken to the skillet. Switch to coat. Serve garnished with parsley.

153 calories per 100g 2g Carbohydrates 9g Fat 692mg Sodium 8g Protein

Tuscan Chicken in a Single Pan Preparation Time: 10 minutes

Time Required for Cooking: 25 minutes

6 portions

Difficult Ingredients: Difficult Difficulty Level: Difficult

14 cup extra-virgin olive oil, divided f 1 pound boneless, skinless chicken breasts, cut into 34-inch pieces f 1 chopped onion f 1 chopped red bell pepper f 3 minced garlic cloves

f 1 can crushed tomatoes, undrained f 1 can chopped tomatoes, drained f 1 can white beans, drained f 12 teaspoon sea salt f 1/8 teaspoon freshly ground black pepper f 1/8 teaspoon red pepper flakes

Directions:

2 tablespoons olive oil should be heated until it shimmers. Cook until the chicken is browned. Remove the chicken from the pan and place it on a serving plate, tenting it with aluminum foil to stay warm.

Re-heat the skillet and add the remaining olive oil. Combine the onion and red bell pepper in a medium bowl. Cook, stirring occasionally, until the veggies are tender. Cook for 30 seconds, stirring regularly.

Stir in the wine and scrape any browned pieces from the bottom of the pan with the side of the spoon. Cook for 1 minute, stirring occasionally.

Combine crushed and diced tomatoes, white beans, Italian seasoning, sea salt, pepper, and red pepper flakes in a medium mixing bowl. Allow to boil for 10 minutes. Cook, stirring periodically, for 5 minutes.

Reintroduce the chicken to the skillet, along with any liquids that have gathered. Cook until the chicken is well cooked. Before serving, remove from the heat and mix in the basil.

Nutritional information (per 100g): 271 kcal 8g Carbohydrates 29g Fat Protein: 14 g Sodium 596mg

Time Required to Prepare Chicken Kapama: 10 minutes Time Required for Cooking: 2 hours 4 Servings Average Difficulty

1 (32-ounce) can chopped tomatoes, drained f 14 cup dry white wine f 2 tablespoons tomato paste f 3 tablespoons extra-virgin olive oil f 14 teaspoon red pepper flakes f 1 teaspoon ground allspice f 12 teaspoon dried oregano f 2 whole cloves f 1 cinnamon stick f 12 teaspoon sea salt f 1/8 teaspoon freshly ground black pepper

Directions:

In a large saucepan, combine the tomatoes, wine, tomato paste, olive oil, allspice, oregano, cloves, cinnamon stick, sea salt, and pepper. Bring to a low heat and cook, stirring periodically. Allow 30 minutes to boil, stirring regularly. Allow the sauce to cool somewhat before removing and discarding the entire cloves and cinnamon stick.

Preheat oven to 350 degrees Fahrenheit. In a 9-by-13-inch baking dish, arrange the chicken. Distribute the sauce evenly over the chicken and tent with aluminum foil. Continue baking until the internal temperature reaches 165°F.

Nutritional information (per 100g): 220 kcal 3g Carbohydrates 11g Fat Protein: 8 g Sodium 923mg

Chicken Breasts Stuffed with Spinach and Feta

Time Required for Preparation: 10 minutes

Time Required for Cooking: 45 minutes

4 portions

Difficulty Average

2 tablespoons extra-virgin olive oil 1 pound fresh baby spinach 3 chopped garlic cloves 12 teaspoon sea salt 1/8 teaspoon freshly crushed black pepper 12 cup crumbled feta cheese 4 boneless, skinless chicken breasts

Directions:

Preheat oven to 350 degrees Fahrenheit. Heat the olive oil in a small saucepan over medium heat until it shimmers. Toss in the spinach. Cook and stir until the spinach is wilted.

Combine the garlic, lemon zest, sea salt, and pepper in a medium bowl. Cook for 30 seconds, continually stirring. Allow it cool somewhat before adding the cheese.

Spread an equal layer of the spinach and cheese mixture over the chicken pieces and fold the breasts up around the filling. Using toothpicks or butcher's twine, secure with toothpicks or butcher's string. Arrange the breasts in a 9circumference around the filling. Using toothpicks or butcher's twine, secure with toothpicks or butcher's string. Bake for 30 to 40 minutes, or until the chicken reaches an internal temperature of 165°F. Remove from oven and let to cool for 5 minutes before slicing and serving.

263 calories per 100g 3g Carbohydrates 7g Fat 639mg Sodium 17g Protein

Baked Chicken Drumsticks with Rosemary

Time Required for Preparation: 5 minutes Time Required for Cooking: 1 hour 6 portions

Difficulty Easy

Ingredients:\sf 2 tbsp. fresh rosemary leaves, chopped f 1 tsp. garlic powder

12 tsp sea salt 1/8 tsp freshly ground black pepper 1 lemon's zest 12 drumsticks de chile

Directions:

Preheat oven to 350 degrees Fahrenheit. Combine the rosemary, garlic powder, sea salt, pepper, and lemon zest in a medium mixing bowl.

In a 9-by-13-inch baking dish, arrange the drumsticks and sprinkle with the rosemary mixture. Bake until the chicken reaches a temperature of 165°F on the inside.

Nutritional information (per 100g): 163 kcal 1 g Carbohydrates 2 g Fat 633mg Sodium 26g Protein

Chicken with Carrots, Onions, Potatoes, Figs, and Fig Juice

Time Required for Preparation: 5 minutes Time Required for Cooking: 45 minutes 4 portions

Difficulty Average

Ingredients:

2 cups fingerling potatoes, halved f 4 fresh figs, quartered f 2 carrots, julienned f 2 tablespoons extra-virgin olive oil f 1 teaspoon sea salt, divided f 14 teaspoon freshly ground black pepper

Directions:

Preheat oven to 425 degrees Fahrenheit. Toss the potatoes, figs, and carrots in a small bowl with the olive oil, 12 teaspoon sea salt, and pepper. Spread the mixture evenly in a 9-by-13-inch baking dish.

Season the chicken breasts with the remaining teaspoon sea salt. It should be placed on top of the vegetables. Bake until the vegetables are tender and the chicken reaches a temperature of 165°F on the inside. Serve garnished with parsley.

Nutritional information (per 100g): 429 calories 4g Carbohydrates 27g Fat 581mg Sodium 52g Protein

Chicken Gyros with Tzatziki Time Required for Preparation: 15 minutes

Time Required for Cooking: 1 hour and 20 minutes

6 portions

Difficulty Average

1 pound ground chicken breast f 1 onion, grated and wrung dry f 2 tablespoons dried rosemary f 1 tablespoon dried marjoram f 6 minced garlic cloves

f 12 tsp sea salt tsp 14 tsp freshly ground black pepper tsp Sauce Tzatziki

Directions:

Preheat oven to 350 degrees Fahrenheit. Using a food processor, combine the chicken, onion, rosemary, marjoram, garlic, sea salt, and pepper. Blend until a paste forms. Alternatively, combine all of these ingredients in a mixing bowl until thoroughly combined (see preparation tip).

In a loaf pan, press the mixture. Bake until the internal temperature reaches 165 degrees. Remove from oven and allow to cool for 20 minutes before slicing.

Slice the gyro and top with tzatziki sauce.

Nutritional information (per 100g): 289 kcal 20g Carbohydrates 1g Fat 622mg Sodium 50g Protein

Moussaka

TEN MINUTES FOR PREPAREATION 45 minutes Preparation Time 8 portion

Difficulty Difficult-to-achieve

5 tbsp extra-virgin olive oil, divided f 1 sliced (unpeeled) eggplant f 1 chopped onion f 1 seeded and chopped green bell pepper f 1 pound ground turkey f 3 minced garlic cloves f 2 tablespoons tomato paste f 1 (14-ounce) can chopped tomatoes, drained f 1 tablespoon Italian seasoning f 2 teaspoons Worcestershire sauce f 1 teaspoon dried oregano f 12 teaspoon ground cinnamon f 1

Pre-heat oven to 400 degrees Fahrenheit. 3 tbsp olive oil, heated until shimmering Cook for 3 to 4 minutes per side with the eggplant slices. Transfer to a draining tray lined with paper towels.

Re-heat the skillet and add the remaining 2 tablespoons olive oil. Add the onion and green bell pepper. Continue cooking until the vegetables are soft. Remove from the pan and set aside. 3. Pull out the skillet to the heat and stir in the turkey. Cook for about 5 minutes, crumbling with a spoon, until browned. Stir in the garlic and cook for 30 seconds, stirring constantly.

Stir in the tomato paste, tomatoes, Italian seasoning, Worcestershire sauce, oregano, and cinnamon. Place the onion and bell pepper back to the pan. Cook for 5 minutes, stirring. Combine the yogurt, egg, pepper, nutmeg, and cheese.

Arrange half of the meat mixture in a 9-by-13-inch baking dish. Layer with half the eggplant. Add the remaining meat mixture and the remaining eggplant. Spread with the yogurt mixture. Bake until golden brown. Garnish with the parsley and serve.

Nutrition (for 100g): 338 Calories 5g Fat 16g Carbohydrates 28g Protein 569mg Sodium

Baked Orzo with Eggplant, Swiss Chard, and Mozzarella

20 minutes for preparation Cooking Time : 60 minutes 4 portion

Difficulty Level : Average\sf 2 tablespoons extra-virgin olive oil\sf 1 large (1-pound) eggplant, diced small f 2 carrots, peeled and diced small\sf 2 celery stalks, diced small\sf 1 onion, diced small\sf ½ teaspoon kosher salt\sf 3 garlic cloves, minced\sf ¼ teaspoon freshly ground black pepper f 1 cup whole-wheat orzo\sf 1 teaspoon no-salt-added tomato paste f 1½ cups no-salt-added vegetable stock f 1 cup Swiss chard, stemmed and chopped small f 2 tablespoons fresh oregano, chopped f Zest of 1 lemon\sf 4 ounces mozzarella cheese, diced small f ¼ cup grated Parmesan cheese\sf 2 tomatoes, sliced ½-inch-thick

Directions:

Preheat the oven to 400°F. Cook the olive oil in a large oven-safe sauté pan over medium heat. Add the eggplant, carrots, celery, onion, and salt and sauté about 10 minutes.

Add the garlic and black pepper and sauté about 30 seconds. Add the orzo and tomato paste and sauté 1 minute. Mix in the vegetable stock and deglaze the pan, scraping up the brown bits. Add the Swiss chard, oregano, and lemon zest and stir until the chard wilts.

Pull out and put in the mozzarella cheese. Smooth the top of the orzo mixture flat. Sprinkle the Parmesan cheese over the top. Spread the tomatoes in a single layer on top of the Parmesan cheese. Bake for 45 minutes.

Nutrition (for 100g): 470 Calories 17g Fat 7g Carbohydrates 18g Protein 769mg Sodium

Barley Risotto with Tomatoes

20 minutes for preparation 45 minutes Preparation Time 4 portion

Average Degree of Difficulty

Ingredients:\sf 2 tablespoons extra-virgin olive oil\sf 2 celery stalks, diced f ½ cup shallots, diced f 4 garlic cloves, minced\sf 3 cups no-salt-added vegetable stock\sf 1 (5-ounce) can no-salt-added diced tomatoes\sf 1 (5-ounce) can no-salt-added crushed tomatoes f 1 cup pearl barley\sf Zest of 1 lemon\sf 1 teaspoon kosher salt\sf ½ teaspoon smoked paprika\sf ¼ teaspoon red pepper flakes\sf ¼ teaspoon freshly ground black pepper f 4 thyme sprigs\sf 1 dried bay leaf\sf 2 cups baby spinach\sf ½ cup crumbled feta cheese\sf 1 tablespoon fresh oregano, chopped\sf 1 tablespoon fennel seeds, toasted (optional) (optional)

Directions:\sCook the olive oil in a large saucepan over medium heat. Add the celery and shallots and sauté, about 4 to 5 minutes. Add the garlic and sauté 30 seconds. Add the vegetable stock, diced tomatoes, crushed tomatoes, barley, lemon zest, salt, paprika, red pepper flakes, black pepper, thyme, and the bay leaf, and mix well. Let it boil, then lower to low, and simmer. Cook, stirring occasionally, for 40 minutes.

Remove the bay leaf and thyme sprigs. Stir in the spinach. In a small bowl, combine the feta, oregano, and fennel seeds. Serve the barley risotto in bowls topped with the feta mixture. Nutrition (for 100g): 375 Calories 12g Fat 13g Carbohydrates 11g Protein 799mg Sodium

Chapter Four

Chickpeas and Kale with Spicy Pomodoro Sauce

TEN MINUTES FOR PREPAREATION Cooking Time : 35 minutes 4 portion

Difficulty Grading: Simple

Ingredients:

f 2 tablespoons extra-virgin olive oil\sf 4 garlic cloves, sliced\sf 1 teaspoon red pepper flakes\sf 1 (28-ounce) (28-ounce) can no-salt-added crushed tomatoes\sf 1 teaspoon kosher salt\sf ½ teaspoon honey\sf 1 bunch kale, stemmed and chopped\sf 2 (15-ounce) cans low-sodium chickpeas, drained and rinsed\sf ¼ cup fresh basil, chopped\sf ¼ cup grated pecorino Romano cheese

Directions:

Cook the olive oil in a sauté pan over medium heat. Stir in the garlic and red pepper flakes and sauté until the garlic is a light golden brown, about 2 minutes. Add the tomatoes, salt, and honey and mix well. Reduce the heat to low and simmer for 20 minutes.

Add the kale and mix in well. Cook about 5 minutes. Add the chickpeas and simmer about 5 minutes. Remove from heat and stir in the basil. Serve topped with pecorino cheese.

Nutritional information per 100g 420 Calories 13g Fat 12g Carbohydrates 20g Protein 882mg Sodium

Roasted Feta with Kale and Lemon Yogurt

15 minutes for preparation. 20 minutes for cooking 4 portion

Difficulty Standard of living:

Ingredients:

f 1 tablespoon extra-virgin olive oil\sf 1 onion, julienned\sf ¼ teaspoon kosher salt\sf 1 teaspoon ground turmeric\sf ½ teaspoon ground cumin\sf ½ teaspoon ground coriander\sf ¼ teaspoon freshly ground black pepper\sf 1 bunch kale, stemmed and chopped\sf 7-ounce block feta cheese, cut into ¼-inch-thick slices\sf ½ cup plain Greek yogurt\sf 1 tablespoon lemon juice

Directions:

Preheat the oven to 400°F. Fry the olive oil in a large ovenproof skillet or sauté pan over medium heat. Add the onion and salt; sauté until lightly golden brown, about 5 minutes. Add the turmeric, cumin, coriander, and black pepper; sauté for 30 seconds. Add the kale and sauté about 2 minutes. Add ½ cup water and continue to cook down the kale, about 3 minutes.

Remove from the heat and place the feta cheese slices on top of the kale mixture. Introduce in the oven and bake until the feta softens, 10 to 12 minutes. In a small bowl, combine the yogurt and lemon juice. Serve the kale and feta cheese topped with the lemon yogurt.

Nutritional information per 100g 210 Calories 14g Fat 2g Carbohydrates 11g Protein 836mg Sodium

Roasted Eggplant and Chickpeas with Tomato Sauce

15 minutes for preparation.

Cooking Time : 60 minutes

4 portion Difficulty Difficult-to-achieve

Ingredients: f Olive oil cooking spray

f 1 large (about 1 pound) eggplant, sliced into ¼-inch-thick rounds f 1 teaspoon kosher salt, divided f 1 tablespoon extra-virgin olive oil f 3 garlic cloves, minced f 1 (28-ounce) can no-salt-added crushed tomatoes f ½ teaspoon honey f ¼ teaspoon freshly ground black pepper f 2 tablespoons fresh basil, chopped f 1 (15-ounce) can no-salt-added or low-sodium chickpeas, drained and rinsed f ¾ cup crumbled feta cheese f 1 tablespoon fresh oregano, chopped

Directions:

The oven should be preheated to 425 degrees Fahrenheit. Grease and line two baking sheets with foil and lightly spray with olive oil cooking spray. Spread the eggplant in a single layer and sprinkle with ½ teaspoon of the salt. Bake for 20 minutes, turning once halfway, until lightly golden brown.

Meanwhile, heat the olive oil in a large saucepan over medium heat. Mix in the garlic and sauté for 30 seconds. Add the crushed tomatoes, honey, the remaining ½ teaspoon salt, and black pepper. Simmer about 20 minutes, until the sauce reduces a bit and thickens. Stir in the basil.

After removing the eggplant from the oven, reduce the oven temperature to 375°F. In a large rectangular or oval baking dish, spoon in the chickpeas and 1 cup sauce. Layer the eggplant slices on top, overlapping as necessary to cover the chickpeas. Lay the remaining sauce on top of the eggplant. Sprinkle the feta cheese and oregano on top.

Wrap the baking dish with foil and bake for 15 minutes. Pull out the foil and bake an additional 15 minutes.

Nutritional information per 100g 320 Calories 11g Fat 12g Carbohydrates Protein - 14g 773mg Sodium

Baked Falafel Sliders

TEN MINUTES FOR PREPAREATION 30 minutes for cooking 6 apports

Average Degree of Difficulty

Ingredients: f Olive oil cooking spray f 1 (15-ounce) can low-sodium chickpeas, drained and rinsed f 1 onion, roughly chopped f 2 garlic cloves, peeled f 2 tablespoons fresh parsley, chopped f 2 tablespoons whole-wheat flour f ½ teaspoon ground coriander f ½ teaspoon ground cumin f ½ teaspoon baking powder f ½ teaspoon kosher salt f ¼ teaspoon freshly ground black pepper

Directions:

The oven should be preheated to 350 degrees Fahrenheit. Put parchment paper or foil and lightly spray with olive oil cooking spray in the baking sheet.

In a food processor, mix in the chickpeas, onion, garlic, parsley, flour, coriander, cumin, baking powder, salt, and black pepper. Blend until smooth.

Make 6 slider patties, each with a heaping ¼ cup of mixture, and arrange on the prepared baking sheet. Bake for 30 minutes. Serve.

Nutritional information per 100g 90 Calories 1g Fat 3g Carbohydrates 4g Protein 803mg Sodium

Grilled Eggplant Rolls

30 minutes for pre-preparation TEN MINUTES FOR COOKING 6 apports

Average Degree of Difficulty

Ingredients: f 2 large eggplants f 1 teaspoon salt f 4 ounces goat cheese f 1 cup ricotta

f ¼ cup fresh basil, finely chopped f ½ teaspoon freshly ground black pepper f Olive oil spray

Directions:

Cut up the tops of the eggplants and cut the eggplants lengthwise into ¼-inch-thick slices. Sprinkle the slices with the salt and place the eggplant in a colander for 15 to 20 minutes.

Scourge the goat cheese, ricotta, basil, and pepper. Preheat a grill, grill pan, or lightly oiled skillet on medium heat. Pat dry the eggplant slices and lightly spray with olive oil spray. Place the eggplant on the grill, grill pan, or skillet and cook for 3 minutes on each side.

Take out the eggplant from the heat and let cool for 5 minutes. To roll, lay one eggplant slice flat, place a tablespoon of the cheese mixture at the base of the slice, and roll up. Serve immediately or chill until serving.

Nutrition (for 100g): 255 Calories 7g Fat 19g Carbohydrates 15g Protein 793mg Sodium

Crispy Zucchini Fritters Preparation Time : 15 minutes 20 minutes for cooking Servings : 6 Difficulty Level : Easy

Ingredients: f 2 large green zucchinis f 2 tablespoons Italian parsley, finely chopped f 3 cloves garlic, minced f 1 teaspoon salt f 1 cup flour f 1 large egg, beaten f ½ cup water f 1 teaspoon baking powder f 3 cups vegetable or avocado oil

Directions:

Grate the zucchini into a large bowl. Add the parsley, garlic, salt, flour, egg, water, and baking powder to the bowl and stir to combine. In a large pot or fryer over medium heat, heat oil to 365°F.

Drop the fritter batter into the hot oil by spoonful. Turn the fritters over using a slotted spoon and fry until they are golden brown, about 2 to 3 minutes. Strain the fritters from the oil and place on a plate lined with paper towels. Serve warm with Creamy Tzatziki or Creamy Traditional Hummus as a dip.

Nutrition (for 100g): 446 Calories 2g Fat 19g Carbohydrates 5g Protein 812mg Sodium

Cheesy Spinach Pies

20 minutes for preparation Cooking Time : 40 minutes 8 portion

Difficulty Difficult-to-achieve

Ingredients: f 2 tablespoons extra-virgin olive oil f 1 large onion, chopped f 2 cloves garlic, minced f 3 (1-pound) bags of baby spinach, washed f 1 cup feta cheese f 1 large egg, beaten f Puff pastry sheets

Directions:

Preheat the oven to 375°F. Warm up the olive oil, onion, and garlic for 3 minutes. Add the spinach to the skillet one bag at a time, letting it wilt in between each bag. Toss using tongs.

Cook for 4

minutes. Once the spinach is cooked, scoop out any excess liquid from the pan.

In a large bowl, mix the feta cheese, egg, and cooked spinach. Lay the puff pastry flat on a counter. Cut the pastry into 3-inch squares. Place a tablespoon of the spinach mixture in the center of a puffpastry square. Crease over one corner of the square to the diagonal corner, forming a triangle. Crimp the edges of the pie by pressing down with the tines of a fork to seal them together. Repeat until all squares are filled.

Situate the pies on a parchment-lined baking sheet and bake for 25 to 30 minutes or until golden brown. Serve warm or at room temperature.

Nutritional information per 100g 503 Calories 6g Fat 38g Carbohydrates 16g Protein 836mg Sodium

Cucumber Sandwich Bites

5 minutes for preparation 0 minutes for cooking 12 portiones

Easy Difficulty

Ingredients: f 1 cucumber, sliced f 8 slices whole wheat bread f 2 tablespoons cream cheese, soft f 1 tablespoon chives, chopped f ¼ cup avocado, peeled, pitted and mashed f 1 teaspoon mustard f Salt and black pepper to the taste

Directions:

Spread the mashed avocado on each bread slice, also spread the rest of the ingredients except the cucumber slices.

Divide the cucumber slices on the bread slices, cut each slice in thirds, arrange on a platter and serve as an appetizer.

Nutritional information per 100g 187 Calories 4g Fat 5g Carbohydrates 2g Protein 736mg Sodium

Yogurt Dip Preparation Time : 10 minutes 0 minutes for cooking 6 apports

Easy Difficulty

Ingredients:\sf 2 cups Greek yogurt f 2 tablespoons pistachios, toasted and chopped f A pinch of salt and white pepper f 2 tablespoons mint, chopped f 1 tablespoon kalamata olives, pitted and chopped f ¼ cup zaatar spice f ¼ cup pomegranate seeds f 1/3 cup olive oil

1. Mix the yogurt with the pistachios and the rest of the ingredients, whisk well, divide into small cups

and serve with pita chips on the side.

Nutritional information per 100g 294 Calories 18g Fat 2g Carbohydrates 10g Protein 593mg Sodium

Time Required to Prepare Tomato Bruschetta: 10 minutes TEN MINUTES FOR COOKING 6 apports

Difficulty Grading: Simple

Ingredients:\sf 1 sliced baguette 1/3 cup basil, finely chopped 6 cubed tomatoes 2 minced garlic cloves 1 teaspoon olive oil 1 tablespoon balsamic vinegar 12 teaspoon garlic powder Spray for cooking

Directions:

Arrange the baguette slices on a parchment-lined baking pan and coat with cooking spray. Bake at 400 degrees for 10 minutes.

Combine the tomatoes, basil, and additional ingredients in a large mixing bowl, stir well, and set aside for 10 minutes. Distribute the tomato mixture evenly among the baguette slices and serve. Nutritional information per 100g 162 kcal 4g Carbohydrates 29g Fat 736mg Sodium 4g Protein

Tomatoes Stuffed with Olives and Cheese

TEN MINUTES FOR PREPAREATION 0 minutes for cooking 24 portions

Easy Difficulty

24 cherry tomatoes, chop tops off and scooping out insides f 2 tablespoons olive oil f 14 teaspoon red pepper flakes

12 cup crumbled feta cheese 2 teaspoons black olive paste 14 cup torn mint In a bowl, whisk together the olive paste and the other ingredients except the cherry tomatoes.

well. Stuff the cherry tomatoes with this mixture and serve as an appetizer. Nutritional information per 100g 136 kcal 6g Carbohydrates 6g Fat 1 gram of protein Sodium 648mg

Time Required to Prepare Pepper Tapenade: 10 minutes 0 minutes for cooking 4 portion

Difficulty Grading: Simple

f 7 ounces chopped roasted red peppers f 12 cup grated parmesan f 1/3 cup chopped parsley f 14 ounces canned artichokes, drained and diced f 3 tablespoons olive oil f 14 cup capers, drained f 1 and 12 tablespoons lemon juice f 2 minced garlic cloves

Directions:\s1. Pulse the red peppers, parmesan, and other ingredients in a blender until fully combined. Distribute evenly among cups and serve as a snack.

Nutritional information per 100g 200 kcal 6g Carbohydrates 4g Fat Protein - 6g Sodium 736mg

Couscous in the Morning Preparation Time: 10 minutes

Time Required for Cooking: 8 minutes

4 portion

Difficulty Standard of living:

Ingredients:

3 cups low-fat milk 1 cup uncooked whole-wheat couscous 1 cinnamon stick

f 12 dried apricots f 14 dried currants f 6 tbsp brown sugar f 14 tbsp salt f 4 tbsp melted butter

1. In a large saucepan, mix milk and cinnamon stick and bring to a simmer over medium heat. 3 minutes in the microwave

minutes, or until microbubbles begin to form around the pan's edges. Avoid boiling. Take the pan off the heat and add the couscous, apricots, currants, salt, and 4 tbsp. brown sugar. Allow 15 minutes for the mixture to rest covered. Take out and discard the cinnamon stick. Distribute couscous evenly among four bowls and top with 1 teaspoon melted butter and 12 teaspoon brown sugar. Prepared for service.

Nutritional information (per 100g): 306 calories 6g Carbohydrates 5g Fat 9 grams protein 944 milligrams sodium

Smoothie with Avocado and Apple Preparation Time: 5 minutes

0 minutes for cooking

Difficulty: 2 Servings Grading: Simple

3 cups spinach f 1 cored, chopped green apple f 1 pitted, peeled, and diced avocado f 3 tbsps. chia seeds

f 1 teaspoon honey f 1 peeled frozen banana f 2 cups coconut water

Directions:

1. In a blender, combine all ingredients. Process until smooth, about 5 minutes, then serve in glasses.

Nutritional information per 100g 208 kcal 6g Carbohydrates 1g Fatty Acid Protein Content: 7g Sodium 924mg

Chapter Five

Mini Frittatas

Time Required for Preparation: 10 minutes

20 minutes for cooking

8 portions Difficulty Grading: Simple

1 yellow onion, chopped f 1 cup grated parmesan f 1 yellow bell pepper, chopped f 1 red bell pepper, chopped f 1 zucchini, chopped Season with salt and freshly ground black pepper. 8 whisked eggs f 2 tbsps. chopped chives

Preheat a frying pan over a medium-high heat. Warm the oil before adding it. Combine all ingredients except the chives and eggs in a large mixing bowl.

Cook for about 5 minutes.

Arrange the eggs in a muffin tin and garnish with chives. Preheat oven to 350 degrees Fahrenheit/176 degrees Celsius. Bake the muffin pan for about 10 minutes. Serve the eggs with sautéed veggies on a platter. Nutritional information per 100g

55 kcal 3 g Carbohydrates 7 g Fatty Acids 844mg Sodium 9g Protein

Tomatoes that have been sun-dried Oatmeal\sPreparation Ten minutes

25 minutes for cooking

4 portion

Difficulty Grading: Simple

3 c. water f 1 c. almond milk f 1 tbsp. olive oil f 1 c. steel-cut oats f 14 c. chopped sun-dried tomatoes A sprinkle of crushed red pepper

Directions:

1. In a saucepan, combine the water and milk. Allow to come to a boil over a medium heat setting. Preheat a second pan over medium-high heat. Warm the oil and cook the oats for 2 minutes. Transfer to the first pan, along with the tomatoes, and stir. Allow around 20 minutes for simmering. Distribute evenly among serving dishes and sprinkle with red pepper flakes. Enjoy.

Nutritional information per 100g 170 kcal 8g Carbohydrates 5g Fat ten grams protein Sodium 645mg

Breakfast Egg on Avocado Time Required for Preparation: 5 minutes

15 minutes total cook time

6 apports

Difficulty Grading: Simple

1 teaspoon garlic powder 12 teaspoon sea salt 14 cups shredded Parmesan cheese 14 teaspoon black pepper 3 pitted avocados, halved

Directions:

Prepare the muffin pans and preheat the oven to 350 degrees Fahrenheit/176 degrees Celsius. Avocados should be split in half. Scrape out about 1/3 of the avocado's flesh to make room for the egg within.

Arrange avocado in a muffin tray so that it faces the topping. Season each avocado with pepper, salt, and garlic powder in an even distribution. Each avocado cavity should include one egg and the tops should be topped with cheese. Bake for about 15 minutes, or until the egg whites are set. Serve and take pleasure in.

252 calories per 100g 2g Carbohydrates 20g Fat Protein 5 g Sodium 946mg

Breakfast Hash with Eggs and Potatoes Preparation Time: 10 minutes

25 minutes for cooking

Difficulty: 2 Servings Grading: Simple

1 diced zucchini f 12 cup chicken broth f 12 pound or 220 g cooked chicken f 1 tbsp. olive oil f 4 oz. or 113 g shrimp 1 chopped sweet potato f 2 eggs

14 teaspoon cayenne pepper 2 teaspoons garlic powder 1 cup fresh spinach

Directions:

Add the olive oil to a skillet. For 2 minutes, fry the shrimp, cooked chicken, and sweet potato. Toss in the cayenne pepper and garlic powder for 4 minutes. Toss in the zucchini for a further 3 minutes.

In a bowl, whisk the eggs and add to the skillet. Season with salt and pepper to taste. Cover the container with the lid. Cook for a further minute, then stir in the chicken broth.

Cook, covered, for a further 8 minutes on high heat. Add the spinach and mix for a further 2 minutes before serving.

Nutritional information per 100g 198 kcal 7g Carbohydrates 7g Fat ten grams protein Sodium 725mg

Soup with Basil and Tomatoes Time Required for Preparation: 10 minutes

25 minutes for cooking

2 Servings Average Difficulty

Ingredients:

2 tablespoons vegetable broth f 1 minced garlic clove f 12 cup white onion f 1 chopped celery stalk f 1 chopped carrot f 3 cup chopped tomatoes 2 bay leaves f 12 cups unsweetened almond milk f 1/3 cup basil leaves

Directions:

In a large saucepan over medium heat, cook the vegetable broth. Cook for 4 minutes before adding the garlic and onions. Carrots and celery should be added at this point. Cook for a further minute.

Bring to a boil with the tomatoes. Reduce to a low heat and simmer for 15 minutes. Combine the almond milk, basil, and bay leaves in a medium bowl. Season with salt and pepper and serve.

Nutritional information per 100g 213 kcal 9g Carbohydrates 9g Fat 817mg Sodium 11g Protein

10 minutes preparation time for butternut squash hummus

15 minutes total cook time

4 portion

Difficulty Grading: Simple

f 2 lbs. or 900 g peeled seeded butternut squash f 1 tbsp. olive oil f 14 c. tahini f 2 tbsps. lemon juice garlic\sf PEPPER, SALT

Directions:

Preheat oven to 300 degrees Fahrenheit/148 degrees Fahrenheit. Drizzle olive oil over the butternut squash. Bake for 15 minutes in the oven, set in a baking dish. After cooking the squash, puree it with the remaining ingredients in a food processor.

Using a food processor, pulse until the mixture is smooth. Carrots and celery sticks are recommended as accompaniments. Place in separate containers, label, and store in the refrigerator for future use. Allow room temperature warming prior to heating in the microwave oven.

Nutritional information per 100g Calories 115 8g Carbohydrates 7g Fatty Acids Protein Content: 10g sodium 946mg

10 minutes for Ham Muffins 15 minutes total cook time 6 apports

Difficulty 9 ham slices f 1/3 cup chopped spinach f 14 cup crumbled feta cheese f 12 cup chopped roasted red peppers f f 112 tbsp. basil pesto f 5 whisked eggs f salt and black pepper

Directions:

1. Coat a muffin tin with nonstick cooking spray. Each muffin mold should be lining with 12 ham slices. Divide the remaining

ingredients into your ham cups, excluding the black pepper, salt, pesto, and eggs. Whisk together in a bowl.

Pepper, salt, pesto, and eggs should all be mixed together. On top, drizzle the pepper mixture. Bake for approximately 15 minutes at 400 F/204 C. Instantaneous service

Nutritional information per 100g Calories: 109 7g Carbohydrates and 8g Fat 386mg sodium 9g protein

Preparation Time for Farro Salad: ten minutes

0 minutes for cooking

Difficulty: 2 Servings Grading: Simple

f 1 tbsp. olive oil f Salt and freshly ground black pepper f 1 bunch chopped baby spinach f 1 pitted and peeled avocado f 2 c. cooked farro 12 c. cubed cherry tomatoes 1 minced garlic clove

Directions:

1. Preheat the oven to a moderate setting. Preheat a skillet with oil. Add the remaining ingredients and stir to combine. Cook the mixture for approximately 5 minutes. Set in serving plates and enjoy.

Nutritional information per 100g 157 Calories 7g Fat 5g Carbohydrates Protein - 6g 615mg Sodium

Cranberry and Dates Squares

TEN MINUTES FOR PREPAREATION

20 minutes for cooking

Servings : 10 Difficulty Grading: Simple Ingredients:\sf 12 pitted dates, chopped\sf 1 tsp. vanilla extract\sf ¼ c. honey\sf ½ c. rolled oats\sf ¾ c. dried cranberries\sf ¼ c. melted almond avocado oil f 1 c. chopped walnuts, roasted f ¼ c. pumpkin seeds

Directions:

Using a bowl, stir in all ingredients to mix.

Line a parchment paper on a baking sheet. Press the mixture on the setup. Set in your freezer for about 30 minutes. Slice into 10 squares and enjoy.

Nutritional information per 100g 263 Calories 4g Fat 3g Carbohydrates Protein Content: 7g 845mg Sodium

Lentils and Cheddar Frittata\sPreparation Time : 5 minutes

Cooking Time : 17 minutes

4 portion

Difficulty Grading: Simple

Ingredients:\sf 1 chopped red onion\sf 2 tbsps. olive oil\sf 1 c. boiled sweet potatoes, chopped\sf ¾ c. chopped ham\sf 4 whisked eggs

f ¾ c. cooked lentils\sf 2 tbsps. Greek yogurt

f Salt and black pepper\sf ½ c. halved cherry tomatoes,\sf ¾ c. grated cheddar cheese

Directions:

Adjust your heat to medium and set a pan in place. Add in oil to heat. Stir in onion and allow to sauté for about 2 minutes. Except for cheese and eggs, toss in the other ingredients and cook for 3 more minutes. Add in the eggs, top with cheese. Cook for 10 more minutes while covered.

Slice the frittata, set in serving bowls and enjoy.

Nutritional information per 100g 274 Calories 3g Fat 5g Carbohydrates Protein - 6g 843mg Sodium

Tuna Sandwich\sPreparation Time : 5 minutes 5 minutes for cooking 2 Portion

Difficulty Grading: Simple

f 6 oz. or 170 g canned tuna, drained and flaked\sf 1 pitted avocado, peeled and mashed\sf 4 whole-wheat bread slices f Pinch salt and black pepper f 1 tbsp. crumbled feta cheese f 1 c. baby spinach

Directions:

Using a bowl, stir in pepper, salt, tuna, and cheese to mix. To the bread slices, apply a spread of the mashed avocado.

Equally, divide the tuna mixture and spinach onto 2 of the slices. Top with the remaining 2 slices. Serve.

Nutritional information per 100g 283 Calories 2g Fat 4g Carbohydrates 8g Protein 754mg Sodium

Denver Fried Omelet\sPreparation Time : 10 minutes

30 minutes for cooking

4 portion

Difficulty Standard of living:

Ingredients:\sf 2 tablespoons butter\sf 1/2 onion, minced meat\sf 1/2 green pepper, minced f 1 cup chopped cooked ham f 8 eggs

f 1/4 cup of milk\sf 1/2 cup grated cheddar cheese and ground black pepper to taste

Directions:

Preheat the oven to 200 degrees C (400 degrees F) (400 degrees F). Grease a round baking dish of 10 inches.

Melt the butter over medium heat; cook and stir onion and pepper until soft, about 5 minutes. Stir in the ham and keep cooking until everything is hot for 5 minutes.

Whip the eggs and milk in a large bowl. Stir in the mixture of cheddar cheese and ham; Season with salt and black pepper.

Pour the mixture in a baking dish. Bake in the oven, about 25 minutes. Serve hot.

Nutritional information per 100g 345 Calories 8g Fat 6g Carbohydrates 4g Protein 712 mg Sodium

Sausage Pan\sPreparation Time : 25 minutes

Cooking Time : 60 minutes

12 portiones

Difficulty Standard of living:

Ingredients:\sf 1-pound Sage Breakfast Sausage,\sf 3 cups grated potatoes, drained and squeezed\sf 1/4 cup melted butter,\sf 12 oz soft grated Cheddar cheese\sf 1/2 cup onion, grated\sf 1 (16 oz) (16 oz) small cottage cheese container\sf 6 giant eggs

Directions:

Set up the oven to 190 ° C. Grease a 9 x 13-inch square oven dish lightly.

Place the sausage in a big deep-frying pan. Bake over medium heat until smooth. Drain, crumble, and reserve.

Mix the grated potatoes and butter in the prepared baking dish. Cover the bottom and sides of the dish with the mixture. Combine in a bowl sausage, cheddar, onion, cottage cheese, and eggs. Pour over the potato mixture. Let it bake.

Allow cooling for 5 minutes before serving.

Nutrition (for 100g): 355 Calories 3g Fat 9g Carbohydrates Protein - 6g 755mg Sodium.

Grilled Marinated Shrimp

30 minutes for pre-preparation

Cooking Time : 60 minutes

6 apports

Easy Difficulty

Ingredients:\sf 1 cup olive oil,\sf 1/4 cup chopped fresh parsley\sf 1 lemon, juiced,\sf 3 cloves of garlic, finely chopped\sf 1 tablespoon tomato puree f 2 teaspoons dried oregano, f 1 teaspoon salt\sf 2 tablespoons hot pepper sauce

f 1 teaspoon ground black pepper,\sf 2 pounds of shrimp, peeled and stripped of tails

Directions:

Combine olive oil, parsley, lemon juice, hot sauce, garlic, tomato puree, oregano, salt, and black pepper in a bowl. Reserve a small amount to string later. Fill the large, resealable plastic bag with marinade and shrimp. Close and let it chill for 2 hours.

Preheat the grill on medium heat. Thread shrimp on skewers, poke once at the tail, and once at the head. Discard the marinade.

Lightly oil the grill. Cook the prawns for 5 minutes on each side or until they are opaque, often baste with the reserved marinade.

Nutritional information per 100g 447 Calories 5g Fat 7g Carbohydrates 3g Protein 800mg Sodium

Chapter Six

Sausage Egg Casserole\s

Preparation Time : 20 minutes

Cooking Time : 1 hour 10 minutes

12 portiones

Average Degree of Difficulty

Ingredients:\sf 3/4-pound finely chopped pork sausage\sf 1 tablespoon butter\sf 4 green onions, minced meat f 1/2 pound of fresh mushrooms f 10 eggs, beaten\sf 1 container (16 grams) (16 grams) low-fat cottage cheese\sf 1 pound of Monterey Jack Cheese, grated f 2 cans of a green pepper diced, drained f 1 cup flour, 1 teaspoon baking powder\sf 1/2 teaspoon salt\sf 1/3 cup melted butter

Directions:

1. Put sausage in a deep-frying pan. Bake over medium heat until smooth. Drain and set aside. Melt the butter in a pan, cook and stir the green onions and mushrooms until they are

soft. 2. Combine eggs, cottage cheese, Monterey Jack cheese, and peppers in a large bowl. Stir in sausages, green onions, and mushrooms. Cover and spend the night in the fridge.

Setup the oven to 175 ° C (350 ° F). Grease a 9 x 13-inch light baking dish.

Sift the flour, baking powder, and salt into a bowl. Stir in the melted butter. Incorporate flour mixture into the egg mixture. Pour into the prepared baking dish. Bake until lightly browned. Let stand for 10 minutes before serving.

Nutrition (for 100g): 408 Calories 7g Fat 4g Carbohydrates 2g Protein 1095mg Sodium

Baked Omelet Squares

15 minutes for preparation Time Required for Cooking: 30 minutes 8 portions

Level of Difficulty: Easy

Ingredients: f 1/4 cup butter f 1 small onion, minced meat f 1 1/2 cups grated cheddar cheese f 1 can of sliced mushrooms f 1 can slice black olives cooked ham (optional) f sliced jalapeno peppers (optional)

f 12 eggs, scrambled eggs f 1/2 cup of milk f salt and pepper, to taste

Directions:

Prepare the oven to 205 ° C (400 ° F). Grease a 9 x 13-inch baking dish.

Cook the butter in a frying pan over medium heat and cook the onion until done.

Lay out the Cheddar cheese on the bottom of the prepared baking dish. Layer with mushrooms, olives, fried onion, ham, and jalapeno peppers. Stir the eggs in a bowl with milk, salt, and pepper. Pour the egg mixture over the ingredients, but do not mix.

Bake in the uncovered and preheated oven, until no more liquid flows in the middle and is light brown above. Allow to cool a little, then cut it into squares and serve.

Nutritional information (per 100g): 344 Calories 3g Fat 2g Carbohydrates 9g Protein 1087mg Sodium

Hard-Boiled Egg Preparation Time : 5 minutes

Time Required for Cooking: 15 minutes

8 portions

Difficulty Easy

Ingredients: f 1 tablespoon of salt f 1/4 cup distilled white vinegar f 6 cups of water f 8 eggs

Directions:

Place the salt, vinegar, and water in a large saucepan and bring to a boil over high heat. Stir in the eggs one by one, and be careful not to split them. Lower the heat and cook over low heat and cook for 14 minutes.

Pull out the eggs from the hot water and place them in a container filled with ice water or cold water. Cool completely, approximately 15 minutes.

Mushrooms with a Soy Sauce Glaze

Time Required for Preparation: 5 minutes Time Required for Cooking: 10 minutes 2 portions

Difficulty Average

Ingredients:

f 2 tablespoons butter f 1(8 ounces) package sliced white mushrooms f 2 cloves garlic, minced f 2 teaspoons soy sauce f ground black pepper to taste

Directions:

1. Cook the butter in a frying pan over medium heat; stir in the mushrooms; cook and stir until the mushrooms are soft and released about 5 minutes. Stir in the garlic; keep cooking and stir for 1 minute. Pour the soy sauce; cook the mushrooms in the soy sauce until the liquid has evaporated, about 4 minutes.

Nutritional information (per 100g): 135 Calories 9g Fat 4g Carbohydrates 2g Protein 387mg Sodium

Dill and Tomato Frittata Preparation Time : 10 minutes

Cooking Time : 35 minutes

6 portions

Difficulty Average

Ingredients:

f Pepper and salt to taste f 1 teaspoon red pepper flakes f 2 garlic cloves, minced f ½ cup crumbled goat cheese– optional f 2 tablespoon fresh chives, chopped f 2 tablespoon fresh dill, chopped f 4 tomatoes, diced f 8 eggs, whisked f 1 teaspoon coconut oil

Directions:

Grease a 9-inch round baking pan and preheat oven to 325oF.

In a large bowl, mix well all ingredients and pour into prepped pan.

Lay into the oven and bake until middle is cooked through around 30-35 minutes.

Remove from oven and garnish with more chives and dill.

Paleo Almond Banana Pancakes Preparation Time : 10 minutes

Time Required for Cooking: 10 minutes

Servings : 3

Average Difficulty

Ingredients: f ¼ cup almond flour f ½ teaspoon ground cinnamon f 3 eggs f 1 banana, mashed f 1 tablespoon almond butter f 1 teaspoon vanilla extract f 1 teaspoon olive oil f Sliced banana to serve

Directions:

Whip eggs in a bowl until fluffy. In another bowl, mash the banana using a fork and add to the egg mixture. Add the vanilla, almond butter, cinnamon and almond flour. Mix into a smooth batter. Heat the olive oil in a skillet. Add one spoonful of the batter and fry them on both sides.

Keep doing these steps until you are done with all the batter.

Add some sliced banana on top before serving.

Nutritional information (per 100g): 306 Calories 26g Fat 6g Carbohydrates 4g Protein 588mg Sodium

Zucchini with Egg Preparation Time : 5 minutes

Time Required for Cooking: 10 minutes

2 portions Difficulty Easy

Ingredients: f 1 1/2 tablespoons olive oil f 2 large zucchinis, cut into large chunks f salt and ground black pepper to taste f 2 large eggs f 1 teaspoon water, or as desired

Directions: Cook the oil in a frying pan over medium heat; sauté zucchini until soft, about 10 minutes. Season the zucchini well.

Lash the eggs using a fork in a bowl. Pour in water and beat until everything is well mixed. Pour the eggs over the zucchini; boil and stir until scrambled eggs and no more flowing, about 5 minutes. Season well the zucchini and eggs.

Nutritional information (per 100g): 213 kcal 7g Fat 2g Carbohydrates 2g Protein 180mg Sodium

Cheesy Amish Breakfast Casserole Preparation Time : 10 minutes

Cooking Time : 50 minutes

12 portions Difficulty Easy Ingredients: f 1-pound sliced bacon, diced, f 1 sweet onion, minced meat f 4 cups grated and frozen potatoes, thawed

f 9 lightly beaten eggs

f 2 cups of grated cheddar cheese f 1 1/2 cup of cottage cheese f 1 1/4 cups of grated Swiss cheese

Directions:

Preheat the oven to 175 ° C (350 ° F). Grease a 9 x 13-inch baking dish.

Warm up large frying pan over medium heat; cook and stir the bacon and onion until the bacon is evenly browned about 10 minutes. Drain. Stir in potatoes, eggs, cheddar cheese, cottage cheese, and Swiss cheese. Fill the mixture into a prepared baking dish.

Bake in the oven until the eggs are cooked and the cheese is melted 45 to 50 minutes. Set aside for 10 minutes before cutting and serving.

Nutritional information (per 100g): 314 Calories 8g Fat 1g Carbohydrates Protein: 7 g 609mg Sodium

Salad with Roquefort Cheese

Time Required for Preparation: 20 minutes

Time Required for Cooking: 25 minutes

6 portions

Difficulty Easy

Ingredients: f 1 leaf lettuce, torn into bite-sized pieces f 3 pears - peeled, without a core and cut into pieces f 5 oz Roquefort cheese, crumbled f 1/2 cup chopped green onions f 1 avocado - peeled, seeded and diced f 1/4 cup white sugar f 1/2 cup pecan nuts f 1 1/2 teaspoon white sugar f 1/3 cup olive oil, f 3 tablespoons red wine vinegar, f 1 1/2 teaspoons prepared mustard, f 1 clove of chopped garlic, f 1/2 teaspoon ground fresh black pepper

Directions:

Incorporate 1/4 cup of sugar with the pecans in a frying pan over medium heat. Continue to stir gently until the sugar has melted with pecans. Carefully situate the nuts to wax paper. Set aside and break into pieces.

Combination for vinaigrette oil, vinegar, 1 1/2 teaspoon of sugar, mustard, chopped garlic, salt, and pepper.

In a large bowl, mix lettuce, pears, blue cheese, avocado, and green onions. Pour vinaigrette over salad, topped with pecans and serve.

Nutritional information (per 100g): 426 Calories 6g Fat 1g Carbohydrates Protein: 8 g 654mg Sodium

Sicilian Kale and Tuna Bowl Preparation Time : 15 minutes

Time Required for Cooking: 15 minutes

6 portions

Difficulty Average

Ingredients: f 1-pound kale f 3 tablespoons extra-virgin olive oil f 1 cup chopped onion f 3 garlic cloves, minced f 1 (25-ounce) can sliced olives, drained f ¼ cup capers f ¼ teaspoon red pepper f 2 teaspoons sugar f 2 (6-ounce) cans tuna in olive oil f 1 (15-ounce) can cannellini beans f ¼ teaspoon ground black pepper f ¼ teaspoon kosher or sea salt

Directions:

Boil three-quarters full of water in a stock pot. Mix in the kale and cook for 2 minutes. Strain the kale with colander and set aside.

Return the empty pot back on the stove over medium heat, and put in the oil. Mix in the onion and cook for 4 minutes, continuous stirring. Place in the garlic and cook for 1 minute. Place the olives, capers, and crushed red pepper, and cook for 1 minute. Lastly, add the partially cooked kale and sugar, stir until the kale is completely coated with oil. Close pot and cook for 8 minutes.

Pull out the kale from the heat, add in the tuna, beans, pepper, and salt, and serve. Nutritional information (per 100g): 265 Calories 12g Fat 7g Carbohydrates 16g Protein 715mg Sodium

Slow Cooker Meatloaf Preparation Time : 10 minutes

Cooking Time : 6 hours and 10 minutes

8 portions

Difficulty Average

Ingredients: f 2 pounds Ground bison f 1 Grated zucchini f 2 large Eggs f Olive oil cooking spray as required f 1 Zucchini, shredded f ½ cup Parsley, fresh, finely chopped f ½ cup Parmesan cheese, shredded f 3 tablespoons Balsamic vinegar f 4 Garlic cloves, grated f 2 tablespoons Onion minced f 1 tablespoon Dried oregano f ½ teaspoon Ground black pepper f ½ teaspoon Kosher salt f For the topping: f ¼ cup Shredded Mozzarella cheese f ¼ cup Ketchup without sugar f ¼ cup Freshly chopped parsley

Directions:

Stripe line the inside of a six-quart slow cooker with aluminum foil. Spray non-stick cooking oil over it.

In a large bowl combine ground bison or extra lean ground sirloin, zucchini, eggs, parsley, balsamic vinegar, garlic, dried oregano, sea or kosher salt, minced dry onion, and ground black pepper.

Situate this mixture into the slow cooker and form an oblong shaped loaf. Cover the cooker, set on a low heat and cook for 6 hours. After cooking, open the cooker and spread ketchup all over the meatloaf.

Now, place the cheese above the ketchup as a new layer and close the slow cooker. Let the meatloaf sit on these two layers for about 10 minutes or until the cheese starts to melt. Garnish with fresh parsley, and shredded Mozzarella cheese.

Nutrition (for 100g): 320 Calories 2g Fat 4g Carbohydrates 26g Protein 681mg Sodium

Slow Cooker Mediterranean Beef Hoagies

Time Required for Preparation: 10 minutes Cooking Time : 13 hours 6 portions

Average Difficulty

Ingredients: f 3 pounds Beef top round roast fatless f ½ teaspoon Onion powder f ½ teaspoon Black pepper f 3 cups Low sodium beef broth f 4 teaspoons Salad dressing mix f 1 Bay leaf f 1 tablespoon Garlic, minced f 2 Red bell peppers, thin strips cut f 16 ounces Pepperoncino f 8 slices Sargento Provolone, thin f 2 ounces Gluten-free bread f ½ teaspoon salt f For seasoning: f 1½ tablespoon Onion powder f 1½ tablespoon Garlic powder f 2 tablespoon Dried parsley f 1 tablespoon stevia f ½ teaspoon Dried thyme f 1 tablespoon Dried oregano f 2 tablespoons Black pepper f 1 tablespoon Salt f 6 Cheese slices

Directions: Dry the roast with a paper towel. Combine black pepper, onion powder and salt in a small bowl and rub the mixture over the roast. Place the seasoned roast into a slow cooker.

Add broth, salad dressing mix, bay leaf, and garlic to the slow cooker. Combine it gently. Close and set to low cooking for 12 hours. After cooking, remove the bay leaf.

Take out the cooked beef and shred the beef meet. Put back the shredded beef and add bell peppers and. Add bell peppers and pepperoncino into the slow cooker. Cover the cooker and low cook for 1 hour. Before serving, top each of the bread with 3 ounces of the meat mixture. Top it with a cheese slice. The liquid gravy can be used as a dip.

Nutrition (for 100g): 442 Calories 5g Fat 37g Carbohydrates 49g Protein 735mg Sodium

Mediterranean Pork Roast

TEN MINUTES FOR PREPAREATION

Cooking Time : 8 hours and 10 minutes

6 apports

Average Degree of Difficulty

Ingredients: f 2 tablespoons Olive oil f 2 pounds Pork roast f ½ teaspoon Paprika f ¾ cup Chicken broth f 2 teaspoons Dried sage f ½ tablespoon Garlic minced f ¼ teaspoon Dried marjoram f ¼ teaspoon Dried Rosemary f 1 teaspoon Oregano f ¼ teaspoon Dried thyme f 1 teaspoon Basil f ¼ teaspoon Kosher salt

Directions:

In a small bowl mix broth, oil, salt, and spices. In a skillet pour olive oil and bring to medium- high heat. Put the pork into it and roast until all sides become brown.

Take out the pork after cooking and poke the roast all over with a knife. Place the poked pork roast into a 6-quart crock pot. Now, pour the small bowl mixture liquid all over the roast.

Seal crock pot and cook on low for 8 hours. After cooking, remove it from the crock pot on to a cutting board and shred into pieces. Afterward, add the shredded pork back into the crockpot. Simmer it another 10 minutes. Serve along with feta cheese, pita bread, and tomatoes.

Nutrition (for 100g): 361 Calories 4g Fat 7g Carbohydrates 8g Protein 980mg Sodium

Chapter Seven

Beef Pizza

Preparation Time : 20 minutes

Cooking Time : 50 minutes

Servings : 10

Difficulty Level : Difficult

Ingredients:\sf For Crust: f 3 cups all-purpose flour f 1 tablespoon sugar f 2¼ teaspoons active dry yeast f 1 teaspoon salt f 2 tablespoons olive oil f 1 cup warm water f For Topping: f 1-pound ground beef f 1 medium onion, chopped f 2 tablespoons tomato paste f 1 tablespoon ground cumin f Salt and ground black pepper, as required f ¼ cup water f 1 cup fresh spinach, chopped f 8 ounces artichoke hearts, quartered f 4 ounces fresh mushrooms, sliced f 2 tomatoes, chopped f 4 ounces feta cheese, crumbled

Directions:

For crust: Mix the flour, sugar, yeast and salt with a stand mixer, using the dough hook. Add 2 tablespoons of

the oil and warm water and knead until a smooth and elastic dough is formed.

Make a ball of the dough and set aside for about 15 minutes.

Situate the dough onto a lightly floured surface and roll into a circle. Situate the dough into a lightly, greased round pizza pan and gently, press to fit. Set aside for about 10-15 minutes. Coat the crust with some oil. Preheat the oven to 400 degrees F.

For topping:

Fry beef in a nonstick skillet over medium-high heat for about 4-5 minutes. Mix in the onion and cook for about 5 minutes, stirring frequently. Add the tomato paste, cumin, salt, black pepper

and water and stir to combine.

Set the heat to medium and cook for about 5-10 minutes. Remove from the heat and set aside. Place the beef mixture over the pizza crust and top with the spinach, followed by the artichokes, mushrooms, tomatoes, and Feta cheese.

Bake until the cheese is melted. Remove from the oven and set aside for about 3-5 minutes before slicing. Cut into desired sized slices and serve.

Nutritional information per 100g 309 Calories 7g Carbohydrates 7g Fatty Acids 3g Protein 732mg Sodium

Beef & Bulgur Meatballs

20 minutes for preparation

Cooking Time : 28 minutes

6 apports

Difficulty Standard of living:

Ingredients:

f ¾ cup uncooked bulgur f 1-pound ground beef f ¼ cup shallots, minced

f ¼ cup fresh parsley, minced f ½ teaspoon ground allspice f ½ teaspoon ground cumin f ½ teaspoon ground cinnamon f ¼ teaspoon red pepper flakes, crushed f Salt, as required f 1 tablespoon olive oil

Directions:

In a large bowl of the cold water, soak the bulgur for about 30 minutes. Drain the bulgur well and then, squeeze with your hands to remove the excess water. In a food processor, add the bulgur, beef, shallot, parsley, spices, salt, and pulse until a smooth mixture is formed.

Situate the mixture into a bowl and refrigerate, covered for about 30 minutes. Remove from the refrigerator and make equal sized balls from the beef mixture. In a large nonstick skillet, heat the oil over medium-high heat and cook the meatballs in 2 batches for about 13-14 minutes, flipping frequently. Serve warm.

Nutritional information per 100g 228 Calories 4g Fat 1g Carbohydrates Protein Content: 5g 766mg Sodium

Tasty Beef and Broccoli Preparation Time : 10 minutes

15 minutes total cook time

4 portion

Difficulty Grading: Simple

Ingredients: i 1 and ½ lbs. flanks steak i 1 tbsp. olive oil i 1 tbsp. tamari sauce

I 1 cup beef stock i 1-pound broccoli, florets separated

Directions: 1. Combine steak strips with oil and tamari, toss and set aside for 10 minutes. Select your instant pot on sauté mode, place beef strips and brown them for 4 minutes on each side. Stir in stock, cover the pot again and cook on high for 8 minutes. Stir in broccoli, cover and cook on high for 4 minutes more. Portion everything between plates and serve. Enjoy!

Nutritional information per 100g 312 Calories 5g Fat 20g Carbohydrates 4g Protein 694mg Sodium

Beef Corn Chili Preparation Time : 8-10 minutes

30 minutes for cooking

Difficulty: 8 Servings Standard of living:

Ingredients: f 2 small onions, chopped (finely) f ¼ cup canned corn f 1 tablespoon oil f 10 ounces lean ground beef f 2 small chili peppers, diced

Directions:

1. Turn on the instant pot. Click "SAUTE". Pour the oil then stir in the onions, chili pepper, and beef; cook until turn translucent and softened. Pour the 3 cups water in the Cooking pot; mix well. 2. Seal the lid. Select "MEAT/STEW". Adjust the timer to 20 minutes. Allow to cook until the timer turns to zero.

3. Click "CANCEL" then "NPR" for natural release pressure for about 8-10 minutes. Open then place the dish in serving plates. Serve.

Nutritional information per 100g 94 Calories 5g Fat 2g Carbohydrates Protein Content: 7g 477mg Sodium

Balsamic Beef Dish Preparation Time : 5 minutes

Cooking Time : 55 minutes

8 portion

Difficulty Standard of living:

Ingredients: f 3 pounds chuck roast f 3 cloves garlic, thinly sliced f 1 tablespoon oil f 1 teaspoon flavored vinegar f ½ teaspoon pepper f ½ teaspoon rosemary f 1 tablespoon butter f ½ teaspoon thyme f ¼ cup balsamic vinegar f 1 cup beef broth

Directions:

Slice the slits in the roast and stuff in garlic slices all over. Combine flavored vinegar, rosemary, pepper, thyme and rub the mixture over the roast. Select the pot on sauté mode and mix in oil, allow the oil to heat up. Cook both side of the roast.

Take it out and set aside. Stir in butter, broth, balsamic vinegar and deglaze the pot. Return the roast and close the lid, then cook on HIGH pressure for 40 minutes.

Perform a quick release. Serve!

Nutritional information per 100g 393 Calories 15g Fat 25g Carbohydrates 37g Protein 870mg Sodium

Soy Sauce Beef Roast Preparation Time : 8 minutes

Cooking Time : 35 minutes

Servings : 2-3

Difficulty Standard of living:

Ingredients:

❖ ½ teaspoon beef bouillon

❖ 1 ½ teaspoon rosemary

- ½ teaspoon minced garlic

- 2 pounds roast beef

- 1/3 cup soy sauce

Directions:

Combine the soy sauce, bouillon, rosemary, and garlic together in a mixing bowl.

Turn on your instant pot. Place the roast, and pour enough water to cover the roast; gently stir to mix well. Seal it tight.

Click "MEAT/STEW" Cooking function; set pressure level to "HIGH" and set the Cooking time to 35 minutes. Let the pressure to build to cook the ingredients. Once done, click "CANCEL" setting then click "NPR" Cooking function to release the pressure naturally.

Gradually open the lid, and shred the meat. Mix in the shredded meat back in the potting mix and stir well. Transfer in serving containers. Serve warm.

Nutritional information per 100g 423 Calories 14g Fat 12g Carbohydrates 21g Protein 884mg Sodium

Rosemary Beef Chuck Roast Preparation Time : 5 minutes

45 minutes Preparation Time

Servings : 5-6

Average Degree of Difficulty

Ingredients: f 3 pounds chuck beef roast f 3 garlic cloves f ¼ cup balsamic vinegar f 1 sprig fresh rosemary f 1 sprig fresh thyme f 1 cup of water f 1 tablespoon vegetable oil f Salt and pepper to taste

Directions:

Chop slices in the beef roast and place the garlic cloves in them. Rub the roast with the herbs, black pepper, and salt. Preheat your instant pot using the sauté setting and pour the oil. When warmed, mix in the beef roast and stir-cook until browned on all sides. Add the remaining ingredients; stir gently.

Seal tight and cook on high for 40 minutes using manual setting. Allow the pressure release naturally, about 10 minutes. Uncover and put the beef roast the serving plates, slice and serve. Nutritional information per 100g 542 Calories 2g Fat 7g Carbohydrates 2g Protein 710mg Sodium

Pork Chops and Tomato Sauce Preparation Time : 10 minutes

20 minutes for cooking

Servings : 4 Difficulty Level : Easy Ingredients:

I 4 pork chops, boneless I 1 tablespoon soy sauce I ¼ teaspoon sesame oil i 1 and ½ cups tomato paste i 1 yellow onion i 8 mushrooms, sliced

Directions:

1. In a bowl, mix pork chops with soy sauce and sesame oil, toss and leave aside for 10 minutes. Set your instant pot on sauté mode, add pork chops and brown them for 5 minutes on each side. Stir in onion, and cook for 1-2 minutes more. Add tomato paste and mushrooms, toss, cover and cook on high for 8-9 minutes. Divide everything between plates and serve. Enjoy!

Nutrition (for 100g): 300 Calories 7g Fat 18g Carbohydrates 4g Protein 801mg Sodium

Dijon and Herb Pork Tenderloin Preparation Time : 10 minutes 30 minutes for cooking 6 apports

Difficulty Standard of living:

Ingredients:

f ½ cup fresh Italian parsley leaves, chopped f 3 tablespoons fresh rosemary leaves, chopped f 3 tablespoons fresh thyme leaves, chopped f 3 tablespoons Dijon mustard f 1 tablespoon extra-virgin olive oil f 4 garlic cloves, minced f ½ teaspoon sea salt f ¼ teaspoon freshly ground black pepper f 1 (1½-pound) pork tenderloin

Directions:

Preheat the oven to 400°F. Blend the parsley, rosemary, thyme, mustard, olive oil, garlic, sea salt, and pepper. Process for about 30 seconds until smooth. Spread the mixture evenly over the pork and place it on a rimmed baking sheet.

Bake until the meat reaches an internal temperature of 140°F. Pull out from the oven and set aside for 10 minutes before slicing and serving.

Nutritional information per 100g 393 Calories 3g Fat 5g Carbohydrates 74g Protein 697mg Sodium

Spanakopita Preparation Time : 15 minutes Cooking Time : 50 minutes Servings : 6 Difficulty Level : Difficult Ingredients: f 6 tablespoons olive oil, divided f 1 small yellow onion, diced f 4 cups frozen chopped spinach f 4 garlic cloves, minced f ½ teaspoon salt f ½ teaspoon freshly ground black pepper f 4 large eggs, beaten f 1 cup ricotta cheese f ¾ cup feta cheese, crumbled f ¼ cup pine nuts

Directions:

Grease baking dish with 2 tablespoons olive oil. Organize the oven at 375 degrees F. Heat 2 tablespoons olive oil in a nonstick skillet over medium-high heat. Mix in the onion to the skillet and sauté for 6 minutes or until translucent and tender.

Add the spinach, garlic, salt, and black pepper to the skillet and sauté for 5 minutes more. Place them to a bowl and set aside. Combine the beaten eggs and ricotta cheese in a separate bowl, then pour them in to the bowl of spinach mixture. Stir to mix well.

Fill the mixture into the baking dish, and tilt the dish so the mixture coats the bottom evenly. Bake until it begins to set. Take out the baking dish from the oven, and spread the feta cheese and pine nuts on top, then dash with remaining 2 tablespoons olive oil.

Return the baking dish to the oven and bake for another 15 minutes or until the top is golden brown. Remove the dish from the oven. Allow the spanakopita to cool for a few minutes and slice to serve. Nutritional information per 100g 340 Calories 3g Fat 1g Carbohydrates 2g Protein 781mg Sodium

Tagine

Preparation Time : 20 minutes Cooking Time : 60 minutes Servings : 6

Difficulty Level : Average

Ingredients:

f ½ cup olive oil

f 6 celery stalks, sliced into ¼-inch crescents

f 2 medium yellow onions, sliced

f 1 teaspoon ground cumin

f ½ teaspoon ground cinnamon

f 1 teaspoon ginger powder

f 6 garlic cloves, minced

f ½ teaspoon paprika

f 1 teaspoon salt

f ¼ teaspoon freshly ground black pepper

f 2 cups low-sodium vegetable stock

f 2 medium zucchinis, cut into ½-inch-thick semicircles

f 2 cups cauliflower, cut into florets

f 1 medium eggplant, cut into 1-inch cubes

f 1 cup green olives, halved and pitted

f 5 ounces (383 g) artichoke hearts, drained and quartered

f ½ cup chopped fresh cilantro leaves, for garnish

f ½ cup plain Greek yogurt, for garnish

f ½ cup chopped fresh flat-leaf parsley, for garnish

Directions:

Cook the olive oil in a stockpot over medium-high heat. Add the celery and onion to the pot and sauté for 6 minutes. Put the cumin, cinnamon, ginger, garlic, paprika, salt, and black pepper to the pot and sauté for 2 minutes more until aromatic.

Pour the vegetable stock to the pot and bring to a boil. Turn down the heat to low, and add the zucchini, cauliflower, and eggplant to the bank. Cover and simmer for 30 minutes or until the vegetables are soft. Then add the olives and artichoke hearts to the pool and simmer for 15 minutes more. Fill them into a large serving bowl or a Tagine, then serve with cilantro, Greek yogurt, and parsley on top.

Nutrition (for 100g): 312 Calories 2g Fat 2g Carbohydrates 1g Protein 813mg Sodium

Citrus Pistachios and Asparagus

Preparation Time : 10 minutes Cooking Time : 10 minutes Servings : 4

Difficulty Level : Difficult

Ingredients:

f Zest and juice of 2 clementine or 1 orange

f Zest and juice of 1 lemon

f 1 tablespoon red wine vinegar

f 3 tablespoons extra-virgin olive oil, divided

f 1 teaspoon salt, divided

f ¼ teaspoon freshly ground black pepper

f ½ cup pistachios, shelled

f 1 pound (454 g) fresh asparagus, trimmed

f 1 tablespoon water

Directions:

Combine the zest and juice of clementine and lemon, vinegar, 2 tablespoons of olive oil, ½ teaspoon of salt, and black pepper. Stir to mix well. Set aside.

Toast the pistachios in a nonstick skillet over medium-high heat for 2 minutes or until golden brown. Transfer the roasted pistachios to a clean work surface, then chop roughly. Mix the pistachios with the citrus mixture. Set aside.

Heat the remaining olive oil in the nonstick skillet over medium-high heat. Add the asparagus to the skillet and sauté for 2 minutes, then season with remaining salt. Add the water to the skillet. Put down the heat to low, and put the lid on. Simmer for 4 minutes until the asparagus is tender.

Remove the asparagus from the skillet to a large dish. Pour the citrus and pistachios mixture over the asparagus. Toss to coat well before serving.

Nutrition (for 100g): 211 Calories 5g Fat 8g Carbohydrates 9g Protein 901mg Sodium

Simple Zoodles

Preparation Time : 10 minutes Cooking Time : 5 minutes Servings : 2

Difficulty Level : Easy

Ingredients:

f 2 tablespoons avocado oil

f 2 medium zucchinis, spiralized

f ¼ teaspoon salt

f Freshly ground black pepper, to taste

Directions:

1. Warm up the avocado oil in a large skillet over medium heat until it shimmers. Add the zucchini noodles, salt, and black pepper to the skillet and toss to coat. Cook and stir continuously, until tender. Serve warm.

Nutrition (for 100g): 128 Calories 14g Fat 3g Carbohydrates 3g Protein 811mg Sodium

Lentil and Tomato Collard Wraps

Preparation Time : 15 minutes Cooking Time : 0 minutes Servings : 4

Difficulty Level : Easy

Ingredients:

f 2 cups cooked lentils

f 5 Roma tomatoes, diced

f ½ cup crumbled feta cheese

f 10 large fresh basil leaves, thinly sliced

f ¼ cup extra-virgin olive oil

f 1 tablespoon balsamic vinegar

f 2 garlic cloves, minced f ½ teaspoon raw honey f ½ teaspoon salt

f ¼ teaspoon freshly ground black pepper

f 4 large collard leaves, stems removed

Directions:

Combine the lentils, tomatoes, cheese, basil leaves, olive oil, vinegar, garlic, honey, salt, and black pepper and stir well.

Lay the collard leaves on a flat work surface. Spoon the equal-sized amounts of the lentil mixture onto the edges of the leaves. Roll them up and slice in half to serve.

Nutrition (for 100g): 318 Calories 6g Fat 5g Carbohydrates 2g Protein 800mg Sodium

CPSIA information can be obtained
at www.ICGtesting.com
Printed in the USA
LVHW060717090922
727942LV00007B/265

9 781837 611218